Printing in Relation to Graphic Art

George French

Alpha Editions

This edition published in 2024

ISBN 9789362514646

Design and Setting By
Alpha Editions
www.alphaedis.com
Email - info@alphaedis.com

As per information held with us this book is in Public Domain. This book is a reproduction of an important historical work. Alpha Editions uses the best technology to reproduce historical work in the same manner it was first published to preserve its original nature. Any marks or number seen are left intentionally to preserve.

Contents

Prefatory Note	- 1 -
Introduction	- 2 -
Art in Printing	- 6 -
Pictorial Composition	- 11 -
Type Composition	- 15 -
Proportion and the Format	- 19 -
Color	- 24 -
Tone	- 29 -
Light and Shade	- 32 -
Values	- 34 -
Paper	- 36 -
Style	- 40 -
The Binding	- 45 -
Specifications	- 49 -

Prefatory Note

It is not the purpose of this book to try to establish a claim for printing that it is an art. It is hoped that it may show that the principles of art may be applied to printing, and that such application may lead to improvement in some essentials of printing.

Thanks are due to several experts in printing who have read the proofs, and have given wise and acceptable counsel.

I desire to acknowledge that aid has been freely sought from books upon art, and that in some instances forms of expression have been adopted from them. No originality is claimed for the allusions to art, nor for art terms and formulas employed.

September, 1903.

Introduction

BECAUSE it is difficult to perfectly transfer a thought from one mind to another it is essential that the principal medium through which such transference is accomplished may be as perfect as it is possible to make it.

It is not wholly by means of the literal significance of certain forms of words that ideas are given currency, whether the words are spoken or printed. In speaking it is easy to convey an impression opposed to the literal meaning of the words employed, by the tone, the expression, the emphasis. It is so also with printed matter. The thought or idea to be communicated acquires or loses force, directness, clearness, lucidity, beauty, in proportion to the fitness of the typography employed as a medium.

It is not primarily a question of beauty of form that is essential in printing, but of the appropriateness of form. Beauty for itself alone is, in printing, but an accessory quality, to be considered as an aid to the force and clarity of the substance of the printed matter.

An object of art illustrating forms and expressions of beauty subtly suggests esthetic or sensuous emotions, which play upon the differing consciousnesses of beholders as their capacities and natures enable them to appreciate it. The impulse received from the art object is individually interpreted and appropriated, and its value to the individual is determined by each recipient, in accord with his nature, training, and capacity.

The motive of a piece of printing is driven into the consciousness of the reader with brutal directness, and it is one of the offices of the typographer to mitigate the severity of the message or to give an added grace to its welcome.

The book has become such a force as had not been dreamed of a generation ago. The magical increase in the circulation of books, by sale and through libraries, is one of the modern marvels. It is inevitable that the gentle and elevating influence of good literature will be greater and broader in proportion to the increase of the reading habit, for despite the great amount of triviality in literature the proportion of good is larger than ever before, and the trivial has not as large a proportion of absolute badness. The critical are prone to underrate the influence of what they esteem trivial literature upon the lives of the people who read little else. It is certain that there is some good in it, and that it affects the lives of those who read it. Even the most lawless of the bandits of the sanguinary novels has a knightly strain in his character, and his high crimes and misdemeanors are tempered with a certain imperative code of homely morality and chivalry. The spectacular crimes are recognized by the majority of readers as the stage setting for the tale—the tabasco sauce for the literary pabulum. They are not considered to be essential traits of admirable character. The cure for the distemper it is supposed to excite resides in the sensational literature of the day; it is as likely to lead to better things, it may be, as it is likely to deprave.

The cultivating power of any book is enhanced if it is itself an object of art. If it is made in accord with the principles of art, as they are applicable to printing and binding, it will have a certain refining influence, independent of its literary tendency.

If we are to subscribe to the best definition of esthetics, we are bound to recognize in the physical character of the books that are read by masses of people a powerful element for artistic education, and one lending itself to the educational propaganda with ready acquiescence and inviting eagerness.

The business and the mechanics of printing have attained a high degree of perfection. The attention bestowed upon the machinery of business, the perfection of systems and methods, has brought commercial and mechanical processes to a degree of perfection and finish that leaves slight prospect of further improvement, more illuminating systems, or more exact methods. The business of printing is conducted in a manner undreamt of by the men who were most consequential a generation ago. Only a few years have passed since the methods that now control in the counting-rooms of the larger printshops were unknown. Now all is system; knowledge, by the grace of formulas and figures.

A like condition prevails in the work rooms: in the composing-room and the pressroom. The processes incident to printing have been improved, in a mechanical way, until little is left for hope to feed upon. The trade of the printer has been broken into specialized units. The "all 'round" printer is no more. In his place there is the hand compositor, the "ad" compositor, the job compositor, the machine operator, the make-up man, the pressman, the press feeder, etc., each a proficient specialist but neither one a printer. To further mechanicalize the working printers, the planning of the work has been largely taken into the counting-room, or is done in detail at the foreman's desk. So every influence has been at work to limit the versatility and kill the originality of the man at the case. The compensatory reflection is the probability that the assembly of results accomplished by expert units may be a whole of a higher grade of excellence.

The process of specialized improvement has been carried through all the mechanical departments, and has had its way with every machine and implement, revolutionizing them and their manipulation also. The time is ripe for a new motive of improvement and advance to become operative. The mechanical evolution may well stay its course. It has far outstripped the artistic and the intellectual motives. It is quite time to return to them and bring them up to the point reached by the mechanics of the craft, if it be found not possible to put them as far in advance as their relative importance seems to demand.

It is not difficult to conclude that certain principles of art have been influential in printing since the craft was inaugurated by Gutenberg and Fust and their contemporaries, but it appears that the relation between printing and the graphic arts has not yet been fully and consciously acknowledged. Some of the older rules and principles of printing are in perfect harmony with the principles and rules of art, and undoubtedly had their origin in the same necessity for harmony that lies in human nature and that was the seed of art principles.

Printing touches life upon so many of its facets, and is such a constant constituent of it, that it requires no special plea to raise it to the plane of one of the absolute forces of culture and one of the most important elements of progress. This postulate admitted, and the plea for the fuller recognition of the control of art principles in printing needs to be pressed only to the point of full recognition, and it requires no stretch of indulgent imagination to find printing successfully asserting a claim to be recognized as an art. It is manifest that printing is not an art in the sense that painting is an art. Painting has no utilitarian side. It is, with it, art or nothing. Printing is 99–100ths utilitarian. It is essentially a craft. If there is a possibility latent in it of development of true art through refinement and reform in its processes, and the application of art principles, to the end that the possibility of the production of occasional pieces that can demonstrate a claim to be art be admitted, it is all that can be hoped. This is claiming for printing only that which is conceded to the other crafts. There is no claim put forward for silversmiths that their work is all artistic; the chief part of it is very manifestly craftsmanship, yet examples that are true art constantly appear. The same is true of wood carving, of repoussé work in metals, and of many crafts. It may be true of printing, and will be when printers themselves become qualified to view their craftsmanship from the point of view of the artist, and feel for it that devotion which is always the recognizable controlling motive of artists in other graphic arts, and in those crafts that verge upon the graphic arts.

Art in Printing

THERE is this vital difference between other objects of art and printing: That our association with them is purely voluntary, and that printing forces itself upon us at all times and in every relation of life. It is impossible for a person of intelligence to remove himself from the influence of printing. It confronts him at every turn, and in every relation of life it plays an important and insistent part.

Such examples of art as a painting or a piece of statuary exert a certain influence upon a restricted number of persons; and it is at all times optional with all persons whether they submit themselves to the influence of such art objects. We are able to evade the influence of other forms of art, but we are not able to ward off printing. To it we must submit. It is constantly before our eyes; it is forever exerting its power upon our consciousness. It is quite possible that we may not at present be able to refer any quality of mind, or any degree of cultivation, directly to printing, in any form it may have been presented to us; but it is easily conceivable that printing has a certain influence upon our esthetic life which has been so constant and so habitual as to have escaped definite recognition.

If we engage our minds in some attempt to realize the quality and extent of pleasure and profit derivable from the constant influence of printing that conforms to artistic principles, we may perceive that it may be a most powerful and effectual agency for culture. It is understood that it is the gentle but constant influence that moulds our habits and lives the more readily and lastingly. If therefore it is possible for us to conceive that the printed page of a book may illustrate and enforce several of the more elemental and important principles underlying graphic art, we may thereby realize that printing may readily be employed in the character of a very powerful art educator, if because of certain inalienable limitations it must be denied full recognition as a member of the sisterhood of arts.

The book page may be regarded as the protoplasm of all printing. If we examine the relation of principles of art to the book page we will be able to appreciate the exact importance of those principles in the composition of any other form of printing, and to so apply them as to secure results most nearly relating printing to graphic art.

It is the chief characteristic of this uncertain dogma of art in printing that its limitations and variations defy the conventional forms of expression, and almost require a new vocabulary of art terms. It assuredly requires a new and a different comprehension of the terms of art, and a distinctly varied comprehension of the word art itself. It has ever been a stumbling block to printers that the word art as applied to their craft must be given a more limited significance than is given it in its usual acceptance. If we can come at some intelligible appreciation of what we mean by art in printing the way will be opened for the application of that motive to the work of the presses.

If we recognize at once the fact that we do not mean exactly what a painter means when we use the word art with reference to printing, we will have taken the vital step toward a comprehensible employment of the term, as well as qualified ourselves for an understanding of the results we desire to achieve.

It is essential that we do not fall into the error of supposing that scientific accuracy is art. It is destructive of art, and the temptation to put too much stress upon exactitude is a mistake the printer must guard himself from with the most sedulous care. It is agreeable to recognize the touch of the artist, in printing as in other arts, and scientific accuracy is certain to obliterate individuality. It is not the cold, lifeless abstraction, the shining exemplar of all the precepts and rules of art, that we love and desire, but the human note speaking through the principles and rules. If the artist is not the dominant note, and the rules submerged by the personality, there is no value in the object of art. The picture is interesting because the artist expresses through it his appreciation, his interpretation, of a beautiful thought or a lovely thing. This is what puts the most faithful photographs outside of the pale of art, and compels the idealization of the performance of the camera before it can be considered to be artistic. The photograph is not, usually, true to our view of life. If it is indeed true to life it represents a view of life that is quite strange to us, and often distasteful. We are not familiar with the uncouth animal the photograph shows us the horse in action to be, and we will not accept that caricature as the real horse. The horse that is real to us is the animal we see with our eyes, and the horse in art must be the animal we see plus the artist's logical idealization. The facts are the same with regard to nearly all of the work of the camera, and with regard to other attempts at scientific accuracy in art. It is foreign to our experience, and does violence to our ideals. We actually see no such automatons as photography shows us men in action are, and we can never accept such disillusionment. If it is attempted in the name of art we will turn upon art and throw it out of our lives.

It is the irredeemable fault of some processes employed in printing that they are too scientifically accurate. This is the legitimate argument against the halftone plate as contrasted with the line engraving or the reproductions of pen-and-ink work, etc. The halftone is too accurate. It brings us face to face with the stark reality, and brushes away all the kindly romance nature has made a necessary adjunct to our powers of vision. Attempts to restore this quality to halftones with the graver are only partially successful, as the defect is too deep seated, too radically fundamental. Some other processes, other than reproductive processes, employed in printing are exposed to this danger of too much scientific accuracy, producing results that have no warmth, no sympathy, no human power. Printing is peculiarly the victim of this cold formality of sentiment, and must be considered as upon that plane. But this fact makes the obligation to be alive to every opportunity to mitigate its severity the more pressing upon every printer who dreams of his work as of an art, and the closer the sympathy between the printer and the culture of art the more warmth and humanity he will be able to infuse into his work.

Some of the principles of art have a fundamental relation to printing, while some have an influence upon it so illusive as to defy definition, and compel us to look upon the connection as something no more substantial than feeling. Indeed, the whole matter of the application of art principles to printing may not unfairly be considered to be one of feeling; involving the saturation of the printer with the rules and tenets of art and the adding thereto of a fine discrimination tempered by a resolute philistinism, and then the play of his cultivated individuality upon the typography.

Principles and rules of art for the printer's guidance must be more mobile than can be permitted for the guidance of the painter, the draughtsman, the engraver, or the sculptor, because the medium for the expression of the printer's conception is so nearly immobile. It is the reverse of the general conception: The rule must adapt itself to the medium and to the circumstances, at least so far as the measure of its observance is concerned, if not in some emergencies where its principle is also at stake. It is conceivable in printing that emergencies may occur making it imperative to ignore the primary rules of composition, of proportion, of balance, or of perspective; it may be necessary to even do violence to principles relating to color or to tone. Such emergencies must be exceedingly rare, but that we are forced to regard them as possible emphasizes the subtle difference between art and art in printing. There can be no good art if the principles of art are violated in execution; there may be good printing if the principles of art are occasionally modified or even ignored.

The motive of printing is not primarily an art motive. It is a utilitarian motive. In printing therefore art is to be invoked for guidance only so far as it will lend itself to the expression of the motive. It is never, in printing, "art for art's sake"; it is ever art for printing's sake. We do not print to illustrate art, nor to produce objects of art. We print to spread intelligence—to make knowledge available to all who will read. A painted picture, if of a high order of art, is meant to appeal to a sentiment but slightly connected with the "story" of the picture. The appreciative observer of a good painting gives little thought to the "story," to the literary motive, but is absorbed in seeking for the artistic motive, in order that he may yield himself to the charm of the work of art; he seeks "art for art's sake."

In printing it is the "story" that is told; it is the literary motive that must be considered, first and most anxiously. Nothing may interfere—not even art. The shaft of the "story" must go, swift and true, straight into the comprehension of the reader. This is the constant anxiety of the printer. The literary motive must not be encumbered. It must be freed from the mechanics of the printed page absolutely. This is the printer's problem. He must not seek to attract to his mechanics. It is the essence of his art that he liberate ideas and send them forth with no ruffled pinions, no evident signs of the pent-house page from which they wing their way.

The printer's work and the painter's art exactly reverse their processes, as their motives are opposed; but they must both work with the same tools, measurably. Everything with the painter is plastic, except his art. Everything is immobile with the printer, except his art; and of that he hopes to employ only so much as will gild the prosaic commercialism of the motive he must express. The chief principles and tenets of art are all applicable to the craft of printing, in some degree. Drawing, composition, harmony, balance, proportion, perspective, color, tone, light-and-shade, values, etc., are qualities of graphic art that apply to printing with varying force, according to the exigencies of each particular case in hand, and particularly according to the comprehension and cultivation of the printer. It is always possible to explain the beauty and power of any piece of printing by reference to the same principles that are responsible for the excellencies of other works of graphic art. It is therefore logical to assume that those principles which explain the excellencies of printing are responsible for them.

It is evident that the value of these art qualities in printing must depend upon the care and intelligence exercised in their application. They are refinements upon the usual and primary practices of printing, and unless they can be employed with full sympathy and knowledge, as well as with the artistic spirit and comprehension, they will appeal to the printer in vain.

The question with the printer is: Is it worth while to give my work all the beauty and distinction and power possible? If it is decided that it is profitable to execute work as worthily as it is possible to execute it, the printer will not be satisfied if he does not devote himself to a study of this phase of his craft, and a study of sufficient breadth and thoroughness to give him a reliable basis of knowledge and the resultant self-confidence. Having proceeded thus far he will not fail to apply all these art tenets to the full extent of his knowledge and their adaptability.

Pictorial Composition

WHILE too much science is often deadly to art, the true basis of pictorial composition is rigidly scientific, and all of the principles governing it are of use and importance to the printer, especially in planning displayed work and in title pages.

Composition is that quality which gives a picture coherence, "the mortar of the wall." It was not esteemed of importance by the old masters, and many of their works do not show that they knew or cared for that which distinguishes a picture from a map, a group photograph, or a scientific diagram. It is the absence of composition, balance, unity, that makes ordinary photographs something other than true works of art. It is not primarily truth of representation that is necessary in a work of art, but truth of idealization; and that quality is beyond the conscious reach of the camera's lens. It is a redeeming and a justifying element added by the imagination of the artist. There may be a picture, by a photographer or by a painter, having all the requisite component parts to make it a work of art; there may be, for example, a woman, an axe, a road, a mountain, trees; but these thrown together upon a canvas do not make a work of art unless they are properly composed, even if they are arranged in an order satisfying to the realist, and each faultlessly executed. It is not the same thing to paint and to make pictures; to print and to execute artistic printing.

The application of the rules of composition to pieces of printing made up in a whole or in part of "display" types is obviously essential to their beauty. It is the touch of beauty given to science that produces art. In printing the matter of securing balance and unity is at once more simple and more difficult than in painting. The component parts to be dealt with are more rigid and restricted, but are purely conventional and precise. The painter's conception is given balance and unity through the original drawing and color-scheme corrected and perfected by constant scrutiny and by tests and continual alterations. The printed piece must be balanced by a wise choice and skilful arrangement of the types, and a careful distribution of white space and black ink, or color. The actual center of a canvas is the center of attraction in a picture perfectly balanced. This does not mean that an equal amount of paint must be spread upon every quarter of the canvas, nor that objects of equal visual importance in themselves must be equally distributed over it. A tiny dot of distinctive paint, placed a certain distance from the center of the canvas, may perfectly balance an object ten times its size which is placed relatively nearer the center. Balance in printing must not be understood to mean that there must be an equal distribution of weight over all quarters of the piece, but that there must be a compensatory distribution of weight.

In his lucid and interesting book upon "Pictorial Composition" Mr. H. R. Poore gives a series of "postulates" which embody his ideas upon the subject, and are expressed in terms intelligible to the non-artistic as well as to those whose familiarity with art enables them to grasp more technical phrases. To the printer it is only necessary to suggest that he interpret "units" as meaning features in his work and he will be able to appreciate that these art rules may not infrequently stand him in good stead, especially when he is perplexed with some piece of work that he is having difficulty in making "look right." Those of Mr. Poore's "postulates" that appear to apply easily to printing, and may be more profitably studied and heeded by printers and others interested in typography, are here given:

All pictures are a collection of units.

Every unit has a given value.

The value of a unit depends on its attraction; of its character, of its size, of its placement.

A unit near the edge has more attraction than at the center.

Every part of the picture space has some attraction.

Space having no detail may possess attraction by gradation and by suggestion.

A unit of attraction in an otherwise empty space has more weight through isolation than the same when placed with other units.

A unit in the foreground has less weight than one in the distance.

Two or more associated units may be reckoned as one and their united center is the point on which they balance with others.

In the application of the rules of composition to graphic art it is possible to minutely subdivide the topic and refer to specific examples and explicit rules for practice. The selection of the particular kind of balance to be sought depends upon the placement of the important item or subject, which is in itself chiefly important in the scheme of balance as giving the keynote, furnishing the starting point. There is the balance of equal measures, which is a picture or piece of printing which may be cut into four equal parts, by horizontal and vertical lines drawn through its center, with each part showing equal weight; the balance of isolated measures, where the chief item is placed away from the center and has one or more isolated spots to compensate, skilfully placed; the horizontal balance; the vertical balance; the formal balance; the balance by opposition of light and dark measures; balance by gradation; balance of isolation, and other varieties of balance more technical and more especially adapted to the painter's uses. Each of these variants of the basic rules of composition may be of special value to the printer, if he studies the subject sufficiently to gain a clear comprehension of how each applies in printing.

This is one of the art subjects that the practical printer may deem of too slight consequence to merit his careful attention. But if it is desired to produce printing of power— power to pleasurably attract the eye of those persons who possess either an instinctive or a cultivated taste for art—it is essential that the work adhere closely to the rules governing pictorial composition. The eye is a relentless judge. Here, as in all printing, the esthetic motive is identical with the business consideration. There is a double motive for the best printing, the esthetic and the business motive, and it is impossible to separate them, or consider either apart from the other. It is unnecessary to attempt to evade the force and meaning of the new appreciation of the basis of good printing, as it leads so surely to financial as well as esthetic betterment, and should be congenial to the tastes of every printer who has advanced in his craft beyond the standards of the wood-sawyer.

Type Composition

THE composition of type is the first task an apprentice is required to undertake when he goes to "learn the trade," and his ideas regarding its importance rarely rise above the level of the drudgery of his early days at the case. But little of the effort to improve the quality of printing has as yet extended back to this primary proceeding, the setting of the type, yet in this fundamental operation lies the possibility for very great improvement and distinction, and for lamentable failure.

Progress in typography has been slower, and it has reached a less advanced position, than have other branches of the printing craft. Presswork for example has become so nearly perfect as to leave little room for the exercise of the critic's art; and the choice and manipulation of paper leaves little hope for radical advance. Type is set as it was set one, two, three generations ago, for the most part. A few printers have given this subject special study, and are executing book pages that are the wonder and despair of the craft. Their distinction has been rather easily won. It is quite possible to detect the source of it, and not difficult to draw the same results from the same fount.

It has become a habit to accept the composed page of type as the foundation upon which to erect a fine piece of printing. The real foundation lies somewhat further back. There can scarcely be distinction in a printed piece unless its source is in the successive steps of progress that antedate the composition of the type. The final artistic result must be clearly conceived in the mind of the printer before he drops one type into the stick. His scheme must be fully developed, and it must be consistent in all its details.

The type for a piece of printing should be selected to give adequate expression to the literary motive, to properly emphasize the subject matter, with the view to the production of a handsome and worthy piece of printing. To secure this latter quality in printing is the primary object of the typesetter, and therein lies the proof of his skill and of his taste. Whether the type selected is the best possible for a given piece of work may be a debatable question, but however it succeeds or fails in this particular, the printer may manipulate it in such a manner as will result in a consistent and artistic example of typography. He may use the sizes which should be in conjunction; he may avoid the common anachronism of lower-case and capital-letter lines in the same piece; he may place his white space so that it will not only be agreeably proportioned to the black or other color of the print but so that it will be as important an element of strength as the ink-covered surface; he may adjust the margins.

These points are all vital, but none of them more so than the use of lower-case and capital-letter lines in conjunction. The capital letters of the ordinary font of type do not lend themselves gracefully to the making of complete words. They are not designed for such work. The lower-case letters are designed to stand together, but it is impossible to combine many capital letters without making noticeable gaps and breaks and some awkward connections. But the objection to capital-letter lines in conjunction with lower-case lines does not rest chiefly upon this point. There are fonts of type from which capital-letter lines scarcely subject to the criticism suggested may be set. The objection is not urged against capital-letter lines in a prohibitive sense, but because their intrusion in a company of lower-case lines destroys harmony. A like deplorable effect is produced by the use of inharmonious series of type for the same piece of typography. The war of styles of type is as destructive to artistic effect as the poorest execution can be. In the old days the apprentice was taught to alternate lower-case and capital-letter lines in job printing, and avoid using two lines of the same series in conjunction.

No one of the small refinements which are now being applied to composition has worked so radical an improvement as the newer ideas relative to spacing, and the perception that the spacing between words, the leading between lines, and the degree of blackness of the face of the letter, must have a balanced relation. This has operated to abolish the conventional em quadrat after the period, and to produce a page of type-matter which lends itself readily to securing tone and optical comfort.

The activity and the fecundity of the type founders in producing new type faces has operated, in the first instance, to furnish new excuse for discord. Then a reaction began, and the liberality of the founders in making complete lines and elaborate series of type faces is suggesting uniformity in scheme and supplying material for consistent execution. The elaborate specimen books are scarcely a temptation to restraint however, nor do they tempt to classicism. Too much type at the hand of the printer is a positive detriment. Until quite recently a very large proportion of the new faces had no warrant for existence. They were abortions, based upon the fantastic ideas of designers who exhibited little knowledge of art or of history. The more recent product of the foundries is much more creditable, and it appears that the designing of type has been taken in hand by artists of capacity, who are actuated by motives worthy of their ambitions and guided by historical research that is true in aim if not always profound.

The typographic tendency is distinctly toward better things. It lags, however. It is not on the level of the other processes of printing. We are yet compelled to admit that presswork is far ahead of composition in development, as is the facility for compounding and handling inks and the selection and the manipulation of paper.

In this vitally fundamental matter we have made little real progress. The disciples of better things are not honored with a following. They are regarded with mild interest by a few of the more progressive ones, with distinct disapproval by the many conservatives, and with utter indifference by the mass. Yet they will win. That there is impending a considerable reform in the composition of type is certain, and the reform will consist in the general adoption of the refinements now practiced by a few: In a closer study of the matter of spacing and leading, with a view to bringing the tone of the page up to near the artistic requirements; in a better balance between body type and chapter and page headings; in a better, more consistent and uniform management of the folio; in order that those features may be actually the guiding and subsidiary features in typography that they assuredly are in the literary scheme of the book.

The time is coming when a book page will be planned to harmonize with and express the literary motive; to promote ease and pleasure in reading; and to satisfy the innate sense of artistic harmony which is felt and appreciated by the cultivated reader, even if, as must often be the fact, he is quite unconscious of the existence of such a demand.

It is upon a basis somewhat like this that books should be planned: Make one page that meets the requirements of art and of the literary motive, and base the book upon it. Such is not the general custom. It is more the fashion to fix the size of the book and accommodate the page to the arbitrary scheme, forcing the type and the format to adequate proportions. There are books that are artistically ruined by the use of type of an inharmonious face, or that may be one size too small or too large; there are many books that are, typographically, abortions, because of neglect to conform to certain very simple tenets of art, when they might as easily have been exemplars of artistic motives and a comfort and delight to each cultivated reader.

It is doubtless because these neglected essentials are so simple and so easily incorporated that it is so difficult to obtain recognition and currency for them. But we may rejoice that books are beginning to receive some of this kind of attention, even in the big printing factories, where books are made very much as barrels of flour are turned out of the great northwestern mills, or as bags of grain are discharged from the modern reapers marching in clattering procession over the horizon-wide wheat townships.

Proportion and the Format

IT IS a delicate and essential matter to fix upon the length of the type page, and a difficult question to fix the margins. There is a mass of literature bearing upon these matters, but they cannot in every case be decided according to arbitrary rules. It is usually safe to be guided by the usual rules in proportioning a page of type, and in placing the page upon the paper. A thorough understanding of the principles of art as they may be applied to printing will suggest occasional infractions of mechanical rules in the interests of good art. Exactly what is to be the procedure in every instance cannot be formulated into rules, but it is always possible to explain justifiable infractions of rules by reference to principles of art. When it is found impossible to thus justify departures from rule, precedent or convention, it is evident that art would have gained if the rules had been adhered to.

The treatment of the format of a book has become somewhat of a moot question, though it is evident that the advocates of the strictly conventional method are gradually drawing practical printers into agreement with them, and that their opponents rely upon the spirit of philistinism for their chief justification, confining their arguments largely to contradiction unfortified by either logic or precedent. Philistinism is not entirely evil, but the present is not a time of such slavish conformity as to clothe it with the appearance of a virtue. Protest is the instinctive spirit of today. In printing there is too much of it. We need more conformity, if conformity be interpreted not to mean blind adherence to precedent but a large and active faith in the saving virtue of demonstrable principles.

Proportion, balance, in a limited sense composition as understood in art, and optics must be considered in adjusting the format of a book. The size and shape of the book must determine the exact dimensions of the page and the margins. The leaf of the ordinary book which is generally approved is fifty per cent longer than it is wide. This proportion is often varied, and for different reasons, but it may be accepted as a standard.

The margins of a correctly printed book are not equal. The back margin is the narrowest, the top a little wider than the back, the front still wider, and the bottom, or tail margin, the widest of all. Why this scheme for margins has grown to be authoritative, and adopted by good bookmakers, is not entirely clear. Nearly all the literature upon the subject is devoted to attempts to justify the custom instead of explaining its origin. The best justification that can now be offered is the evident fact that the custom is agreeable to publishers, to authors, and to discriminating readers.

It is often alleged that there is some law of optics that is in agreement with the custom, but it might be difficult to establish such a claim though it is not necessary to attempt to refute it. We are accustomed to this arrangement of the margins in the best books, and that to which we have become accustomed requires no defense, scarcely an explanation. It is certain that the format of a book appeals to us as right only where this arrangement of unequal margins is strictly observed. It is easy to imagine that our eyes rest more contentedly upon the pair of pages before them when those pages incline toward the top of the leaves and toward each other. The eye of the bookish person is undeniably better satisfied if the margins are proportioned as specified. There may be grounds for doubting the claim that the reasons for such satisfaction are optical; there are some plausible arguments to support such a contention. It is a question for oculists.

The other reasons for the evolution of the book format into its present form are logical. If they do not lead to the conclusion that art has been served and justified in full they assuredly do not lead to a contrary conclusion. The early paper makers produced a sheet that was uneven in shape and variable in size, and the pressman was compelled to make large allowance on the front and tail margins. The back and top margins could be reckoned, as when the sheet was folded by the print they would be uniform. The front and tail margins were made wide enough to allow for the unevenness of the paper and for the trim. It was inevitable that the allowance should be too great, and that to preserve the proper form and proportion for the book the front and tail margins should occasionally be left wider than the back and head margins. This, it may be imagined, did much to fix the present custom. The ancient handmade papers were thicker on the fore edge of the sheet than in the center, and as the bookbinder could not beat the edges flat they had to be trimmed off.

In the old days books were taken more seriously than they now are, and studious readers desired to annotate their copies of favorite books. The front and tail margins were used for this purpose, and they were therefore given their larger proportion of the sheet. In the fifteenth century this motive for wide margins was recognized by all printers, and many of them went so far as to provide printed annotations for all four of the margins.

There were other motives for fixing the margins as we have them. Whether the optical and the artistic motives, purely as such, may explain the modern format more logically than the historical motives do, may be debatable. The question is not vitally important. We wish to see the format of our books made as the best practice makes it, whether our taste is inherited as a habit or is acquired through our artistic cultivation.

Accepting therefore the dictum as it stands, without pressing an inquiry as to its authority or its legitimacy, it remains something of a problem to fix the margins and place the page of a book. When all suggestions and rules are considered it will be found that it is not often that the ordinary book page will submit gracefully to variation of the rule that the length be determined by cutting the page into two triangles, the hypotenuse of either of which shall be twice the width of the page. The page-heading should be included in this measurement, but if the folio is placed at the foot, either in bare figures or enclosed within brackets, it need not be included. This formula must often be disregarded, especially when the book is not to be proportioned in conventional dimensions. No other form is as satisfactory however, and it is quite within the bounds of the practice of the better bookmakers to consider it as the approved conventional page. Whenever it is varied the guide must be a general sense of appropriateness, having consideration for all the other varied elements.

There are other rules. One that was much in vogue at one time, and is esteemed now by some good printers, makes the type page one-half more in length than its width. This rule is restricted in its application. It will not do for a quarto page, nor for a broad octavo. Another rule provides that the sum of the square inches on the back and top margins shall be one-half the sum of the square inches on the front and tail margins. This is difficult to apply in practice, for obvious reasons, except as a test to determine the correctness of margins already fixed.

The margins must be adjusted with the intent to make the two pages lying exposed to view properly harmonize with the book leaf, and adjust themselves to the tyrannical optical demands of the eyes of the reader. This requires a very strict and careful adherence to rules well understood by good printers, as well as a courageous disregard of those rules when the exigencies of the case demand it. There are many other things to consider. The general character and purpose of the book must be taken into account, the size of type, and whether it is to be leaded or set solid, the quality and weight of paper, etc. A bible, guide book, or directory, need not have wide margins, nor a book printed on small type and thin paper; and a book the type for which is not leaded should be given less margin than is allowed for a page of leaded type. While the same general scheme for margins is applicable to nearly all good books, of whatever shape and size, when the contents and object do not dominate the physical character, it is obvious that the dimensions cannot in all cases be fixed according to the same formulas. A quarto page must have wider margins than an octavo, but they must bear a like relative proportion to each other. A quarto page must be proportioned differently than an octavo; it must be shorter by about one-seventh.

The width of the margins must in some degree depend upon the amount of white in the page of type, upon the tone of the type page. This involves the character of the type face quite as much as the spacing and leading given it, as some type faces have such light lines as to give the page a very light tone, even when the type is set solid and the spacing is close, other types have such heavy lines as to demand wide spacing, leading, and wide margins, to bring the tone down to a proper degree of grayness.

Consideration of all these questions affecting the format, and especially the margins, of a proposed book lead to the conclusion that it is good practice to select the paper as the first step in the planning of a book that is intended to be made upon artistic lines, and upon this foundation to build the typography and the binding, according to the rules of harmony and of proportion.

Color

IN art, color is not essential to some forms and processes, as engraving, etching, charcoal work, and the various forms of crayon work; and in printing, it is absent from the large percentage of work done in black and white.

This limitation of the application of the word "color" in printing is quite arbitrary. If we speak in the strictest sense we must consider that black and white work is color work. White is the concentration of all the rays of the solar spectrum, the epitome of all colors; while black is the appearance of the substance that most nearly rejects all reflections of the spectrum colors; and black and white are as truly colors as are red, violet, vermilion, or any of the other brilliant tints. Yet as it is usual to allude to black and white as some other qualities than color, and as they affect us so differently, it is deemed to be more convenient to consider them in relation to light and shade, tone, and values, and to confine the meaning of "color" to the tints shown by the spectrum. This is not an insignificant distinction when employed in relation to printing, as much of the beauty and power of the plainly printed book page is due to the apportionment of black and white—black type and white paper. So when we speak of color in printing it must be understood that the word is not used in its broadest, nor in its most exact, sense; but in an arbitrarily restricted sense, applying exactly as it is applied by printers in actual practice.

The printer's understanding of color, his appreciation of its usefulness and power, is approaching toward the high esteem in which it is held by the painter. He is coming to know that it is a high quality of his work, and that by it he is able to suggest several other qualities that are vital, such as lights, shadows, perspectives, etc.

There are no explicit rules for the guidance of the printer in the use of color. There are certain fundamental principles, and many rules deduced from them, a thorough acquaintance with which will enable him to avoid serious blunders and greatly aid him in the working out of a scheme; but that sense of rightness which the successful artist or craftsman occasionally experiences, cannot be won by the mere following of the letter and the spirit of rules. How true this is becomes apparent when the work of the best printers is examined with intelligent care, and it seems absolute when the meager list of great painter colorists is reviewed: Titian, Giorgione, Tintoretto, Paul Veronese, Rubens, Velasquez, Delacroix, and a few with less claim to the title. All that is known about color has been absorbed by hundreds of artists; yet out of a great army of successful students there have come so few good colorists that their names can be spoken in ten seconds.

To effectively deal with color a fair understanding of what science is able to tell of its essential properties and powers is necessary as a basis. To this may be added such of the deductions and rules as have been formulated by the great painters and the students.

The important starting point is this: To realize that color is not a material existence, not a substance, not a fixed fact equally appreciable by all and equally demonstrable to all. It is a sensation; and a sensation not of the same force or quality for different individuals. Of itself it depends upon the waves of the ether in space; for us it depends upon the power and truth of our eyes. One may truthfully see a color that is quite another thing to another person, if there should chance to be a difference radical enough or defects serious enough in the eyes of either. The laws governing light are of great importance to the colorists. There are subtleties that have important practical application which cannot be guessed otherwise than by direct reference to science. In no other way can a printer know for example what colors are complementary or what effect a certain color will have upon another when they are used together.

There are many curious facts about color which do not appear to be regulated by laws at all similar to those we are accustomed to apply in other matters; that there is this universal and radical difference is of great importance to those who use color in printing. It is interesting to realize that color is produced by light waves, the different colors by waves of different lengths, or greater frequency; that red appears to the eye when the light wave is 1/39000 of an inch in length, or when the frequency of the vibration is 392 quadrillions per second, by the American system of enumeration. It may be also of practical money value to the printer to know such facts, and to always be conscious of a fact more likely to be of practical use, namely, that the sensation of color is produced upon our sensory nerves in a manner closely analogous to that which produces the sensation of harmony: by ether waves set in motion in a different way. These sensory nerves are the most easily entered avenues to our pleasurable sensations; far more delicate and responsive than the different brain organs to the more obvious consciousnesses, as personal regard and literary appreciation, etc.

The printer handling color is making an appeal of the most subtle and delicate nature, vastly more so than is made by the type matter that may form the body of the piece of printing he is embellishing with color.

There are three primary colors—red, yellow, and blue—and three composite colors, which can be formed by mixings of primary colors—green, orange, and violet. It is of importance to the printer to know which of these colors are complementary and which uncomplementary. Complementary colors are those that may be used in close conjunction without one unfavorably affecting the other. This is the secret of complementary, or harmonious, colors: Will they make white if mixed? This means a natural and perfect union of the light rays reflected from the color scheme upon the eye's retina, and so passed along to the sensory nerves—the telegraph line from the physical world to the appreciative brain. It appears that those complementary color schemes which can be perfectly justified are such as reflect light rays nearest like the rays that show us white. Red and green, the two most pronounced and vigorous colors, are complementary. When mixed in the proper proportions they produce white, but this does not mean that they weaken each other when otherwise used; when placed side by side they enhance each other's power and brilliancy by reflection. Their very intimate relation is further shown by the fact that red, by itself, is bordered by a faint halo of green, and green by a tinge of red. Yellow and indigo also make white by mixing, and easily reveal traces of each other when properly manipulated. This interchange between complementary colors is carried still further: The shadow of a color does not show the color itself, but the complementary color to which it is most nearly related.

There is a curious law of optical mixture to deal with—that tendency of the eye to unify the color scheme which changes colors when used in combination upon a piece of printing or upon a canvas. This sometimes so changes the expected effect of a color scheme that has been carefully studied as to render it inadvisable to use it. It is generally found that optical mixture verifies the taste and judgment of the colorist who has been faithful to the complementary color laws, and helps him to a harmony, rather than condemns his work. Optical mixture is too nearly a mere name for a manifestation of the relation of complementary colors to trouble the printer, though a consciousness of it and its effect may at times aid him in producing some delicate effects.

The reasons for desiring reliable knowledge of these qualities of colors are clear. Brilliancy is obtained by using complementary colors side by side, because each gives to the other its favorable halo of color; and dulness of coloring follows the use of uncomplementary colors side by side because each partially kills the other with its unfavorable halo of color.

Careful observance of this law of colors will not give perfect harmony to the color scheme, but it will give one of the more important elements of harmony. But there is an important exception to be noted. The law of contrast claims attention, though it cannot produce harmony. Strong effects may be obtained by ignoring these rules relative to harmony, or by boldly employing pronounced discords and seeking to so mitigate the discord as to tempt the attention to divide itself between the contrasting colors. Red and blue in the national flag are so tempered with pure white as to subdue their fierce antagonism. And so it may be with other examples—there must be either some overpowering sentiment or some skilful expedient, like breaking the main colors into lower tints, to ease the transit from one to the other. A good piece of color work need not be composed of different colors. It may be composed of different shades of the same color, or of tints very nearly related. This requires a good workable knowledge of perspective and of that rather elusive and indefinite quality known in painting as "values"; which chiefly means that each tint employed in a piece of work shall be placed as it would appear in nature and shall properly harmonize with every shade or color in the piece. Such a composition as this is difficult for a letter-press printer, less so for a lithographer, with exactly the kind of delicate manœuvering that delights some painters. It involves such fine discriminations as are necessary to show the difference between a white handkerchief and white snow, between a gray house and a gray sky, between a green tree and a green mountain, between a carnation pink and a pink muslin gown.

It is well to appreciate the difference between color and colors, and to recognize the fact that good color does not necessarily alone mean the degree of brightness or contrast, but is oftener found in accordance, mellowness and richness. Color does not always mean bright color. There is beginning to be seen some low keyed color work, simple in color composition. It is a good sign. It is only the masters who are able to successfully cope with the high keyed compositions, and the masters are, as they ever were, scarce.

The wise choose, when there is a choice, such harmonies as may be indicated by mahogany wood and Cordova leather; Indian red instead of brick red, peacock blue instead of sky blue, olive green instead of grass green; golden browns, garnet reds, Egyptian yellows, deep tones of brown, green, and orange. These colors are not gay, flippant nor flimsy; they are dignified and good style; they have a quality of beauty inherent in them—a depth; and they may be in keeping with a motive in the printed piece that means something other and better than a shock to the color sense.

Tone

NO quality of printing is of more general importance than tone. It has great weight as a purely artistic attribute, and it has a great physiological value. If the tone of a page of print is not right—if it does not conform very closely to the standard set up by the rules of art—it will not be "easy" reading, and will severely try eyes that are not absolutely normal and perfectly strong. Here as elsewhere, and as is the unvarying rule, the art standard is the standard required by hygiene and common sense.

It is of the greatest importance that a printed page shall be toned, with respect to the proportion of visible white paper and black type, in strict accord with the requirements of art, which are identical with the rules that guard healthy eyesight.

Tone in painting has a radically different meaning in America from the meaning attached to the term in England and in France, and it appears to be less important. The American meaning of the word tone as an element in painting is that it refers to the dominant color of a picture; that is, as one would note that the prevailing color of a certain picture is red, of another yellow, of another blue. This makes of tone a mere descriptive adjective of small value as an aid to a critical estimate or as a guide in creation. To the printer, this meaning of the term would bar it out of his curriculum. The English understanding of tone is quite different, and it appears more worthy of acceptance. It is, at all events, the meaning that must be accepted by printers if they are to derive any benefit from a study of tone as a possible aid in their craft. The English consider tone to be "the proper diffusion of light as it affects the intensities of the different objects in the picture; and the right relation of objects or colors in shadow to the parts of them not in shadow and to the principal light."

It is easier, and may be clearer, to think of tone in a piece of type composition, or in a black-and-white engraving prepared for printing, somewhat as we think of tone in music. And we find upon getting further into the subject that it is expedient to take advantage of the extreme comity at present existing between England and America and let the two meanings of tone merge into a more general one for the benefit and use of the printer in practice. The painter's estimate of the tone of a painting may be understood by applying a test cited by a writer upon art: "If the canvas were placed upon a revolving pin and whirled rapidly around, the coloring would blend into a uniform tint." The color tone of a painting must then be the dominant color, modified by the subordinate colors. If the color tone be yellow for example, as it is in some of the good work of Dutch artists, there must be enough yellow so that it will be a yellow blur if the piece is spun rapidly around.

In black-and-white printing tone must mean depth of color, and diffusion of color, and the tone can scarcely be otherwise than some shade of gray. If it is advantageous to strive for a certain harmony between literary motive and type motive an appreciation of the technical meaning of tone and the utilization of the unique test suggested may be of great assistance to the printer of black-and-white work.

The printer has to consider the tone of his piece in a different light than the painter. The latter has only his canvas to take account of, and he works his canvas to its edge. The printer has his page of type and his margins. This blends the question of tone in a very practical way with questions bearing upon the format—with the question of proportion for example, and with the important question of the balance of the margins; and while the determination of the tone of the type page itself, irrespective of the margins, involves one weighty question in optics, the placing of the type page upon the leaf involves another, quite different in nature but none the less important from an artistic point of view.

It is easily perceived that the element of tone is of considerable importance in what is erroneously called "plain" composition, the black-and-white book page. In color printing it is apparent that the knowledge of tone is of more practical importance, as colored printed pieces should show a decided preponderance of that tone which best illustrates or translates the idea that the piece is conceived for the purpose of expressing. It may be important that a certain piece emphatically presents to the eye a certain shade of red. It must be just enough given over to the red to produce the effect required—no more, no less. There must be red everywhere, but not too much. The simple test will show the printer whether he is overloading his piece with the dominant color or whether he has not yet used enough. The color scheme must be keyed to the required pitch of color, as a piece of music written in a certain key must be kept free from notes belonging to another key. But not absolutely free, of necessity; short notes of another key, and very few of them, may be introduced. So a touch of a radically different color may be thrust into a composition without ruining it, as a bit of brick red or small patch of blue in a monotone, or a little green or yellow in a red composition, but not enough to show plainly when we apply the whirling test.

This more obvious meaning of the term tone seems to be applicable to printing, at least to the extent of informing and modifying the mind of the printer. The more important significance of the term in painting means but little to the printer, as it deals in modifications and gradations in color not practicable in typography, and applying, so far as printing in general is concerned, to engravings.

Light and Shade

LIGHT and shade means nearly the same as the English idea of tone, to the printer, as it has to do with the distribution of light and shadow in such a manner as will best illustrate the motive of the painter. This important element in graphic art has its value for the printer. It is only necessary to note the part played by light and shade—"light-tone"—in any work of art to conceive how important is its office in good printing, particularly in the printing of the modern process engravings. Some of the older Japanese and Chinese paintings are nearly devoid of light and shade, and are therefore given that appearance of flatness and false perspective which is their distinctive characteristic. Egyptian and Assyrian wall painting, and many Italian paintings of the medieval period, lack this quality, and they sharply emphasize its importance in graphic art. In nature it is more important than in art. We can recognize no form except by the aid of light and shade, neither a grain of sand nor a mountain, nor any other physical thing. It is probable that every piece of good printing owes some of its excellence to this element of light and shade; and as directly to tone. Light and shade has reference to the proper proportion of light to shadow, and of shadow to light; not to the proper proportion of light to shade in a composition. That is tone. Is there light enough to supplement the shadow, and thus bring the object illustrated into such reasonable harmony with nature as to warrant us in accepting it as a faithful picture of nature? Does the composition, in other words, appear natural to an untrained vision?

It is the persistent study of this question of light and shade which has rescued the halftone engraving from the pit of oblivion into which it seemed destined to fall during its early days, and placed it in the forefront of illustrative processes. Probably the halftone of today, which in competent hands is a superb and exact recorder of nature, is not strikingly better in any other detail than it was in its early days except the one quality of light and shade. This variety of illustration was as flat and as expressionless as a Chinese painting until artist, engraver, and printer conspired to give it expression and verisimilitude by working up its capacity to bring light and shade fully and broadly to its task. There can be no rule that will apply to this employment of light and shade. Rules there are, but they apply with truth only to one experience—that which prompted their formulation. The eye of the printer is the guide. This is the reason why he should study this question, and others of similar artistic value, from the point of view of the artist, not from the viewpoint of the printer.

Values

THE quality in a painting which is known as "values" may quite easily be regarded by the printer as signifying to him the same as tone. Careful study will show him that there is a difference, and also that value is a vital element in his work which has for him a real significance. Value may not unfairly be considered to be an element of tone. It relates to the intensity of light; not the brilliancy of color, but the capacity that resides in color to reflect light. In color printing the value of the most common colors ranks with yellow first, then orange, green, red, blue, and violet. That is, yellow is capable of reflecting more light from the same quantity of sunlight than any other color, and violet less than any other color. Scientists have reckoned that chrome yellow reflects 80 per cent of light, green 40 per cent, etc. These figures serve no very practical purpose, because the reflecting power of any tint is dependent upon the other colors employed. Colors are dependent upon each other for their value as well as for their intensity and their harmony. It is not difficult to treat this matter of value in a mathematical way, as is suggested by Prof. J. C. Van Dyke: "Let the chrome yellow with its 80 per cent of light represent a sunset sky in the background; let the green with its 40 per cent represent the grass in the immediate foreground; and let the orange-red with its 60 per cent represent the sail of a Venetian fishing vessel upon the water of the middle distance. Now we have the three leading pitches of light in the three planes of the picture," and the problem would stand thus: 40:60::60:80 and the result will indicate the relative power of the value in the picture.

Interesting, but not especially useful, the "practical" printer says. No, not unless there is recognizable in this, as in all that has been said about art in printing, the subtle relation between the vital elements of graphic art and those refinements of knowledge and practice which tend to bring printing nearer to the arts. The connection is there, and is evident to the seeing eye. In nature and in life the sense of values is of such importance that without it objects would not have relative positions; all would be a jumble of shades and tones, objects and colors; we would stumble, as we could not see depressions; we would grasp an arm or the empty air, when we attempted to seize a hand; we could not judge distances. It is upon the extent and the thoroughness of the printer's knowledge of this question of values that the degree of refinement and truth he is able to impart to a certain class of work depends, and hence its money value to him and its intrinsic value to his patrons.

Paper

PAPER is as important an artistic or esthetic element in the well-made book as it is as a technical element; and it is likewise to be regarded from the point of view of the optician and the physiologist.

It is possible to select a paper for any book that will lend itself to the artistic scheme of the book. It has not long been possible to do this. The product of the skilled paper maker has more than quadrupled, in artistic variety, during the few years last past, until it is now the fault of its designer if a book intended to be harmoniously artistic is not as true to its motive in paper as in typography or binding. But it is evident that paper for a book cannot be selected without reference to the typography, the plates, and other mechanical features. A grade of paper that would be appropriate for the printing of a rugged-faced type (like Caslon) upon, would not do at all for a conventional type, such as the Scotch face, it might be discovered, even though the paper, in texture and finish, seemed to be peculiarly appropriate for the literary motive. There are certain type faces which may be printed upon paper that is milk white, and certain other faces that lend themselves more readily to the production of harmonious tonal effects when the paper has a "natural" tint, or is thrown strongly toward a brown color. Either of these combinations, or any similar combination, may harmonize unfavorably with the literary motive, or with the scheme for proportion and balance, or with the tone and values element, and though admirable in itself have to be finally rejected.

The weight and texture of the paper have to be considered as minutely and as carefully, and with the same principles in full view. A delicate and shy literary motive must not be given the massive dignity of heavy handmade paper and large and strong type. Such a scheme is harrowing to a sensitive reader's nerves and rudely subversive of the more obvious and elemental artistic principles.

It is a complex and an involved process to select the proper paper for a given piece of printing, and the rightful decision of either of the component elements involves the rightful decision with reference to each of the others. It is impossible to consider the question of paper apart from a consideration of the typography, the illustrations, the format, and the binding; and it is not possible to consider either of these elements apart from the literary motive, which must always be the foundation of the structure.

Paper is one of the group of coördinately important elements in a piece of artistic printing, and only one, and never otherwise than strictly coördinate. It may not be considered by itself, unless possible disaster be consciously and deliberately invited.

Therefore before the specifications for a book or other piece of printing are otherwise fixed, it is necessary to decide upon the paper to be used. It is one of the elements of printing over which the printer exercises no control except the liberty of choice. He can choose the paper he wishes to use, but he cannot adapt it. He can adapt his typographic plan and his color scheme, and adjust them to the paper in such fashion as will result in harmony for the completed work, but his paper he is obliged to take as the paper-maker furnishes it. For this reason, and because the paper is actually a foundation element in printing, it is necessary that printers know about paper, and that those who essay to execute work of a high standard be familiar with its history, composition, and methods of manufacture.

Too much importance will not be likely to be attached to the history of paper, for it runs parallel with the record of the advance of civilization and learning, and it has been an indispensable factor in that advance. When we note the important part played by paper in the complicated scheme of our twentieth century lives, we may gain some faint appreciation of its place and relative importance as a factor of life. As a factor in printing it has been customary to place paper first in the list. It is a safe practice, though the versatility of the paper makers is yearly making it less essential to do so. Yet, when all the progress in paper making has been considered, it paradoxically remains that the selection of paper by the printer is not the simple matter it was only a few years ago.

With the progress of the art of printing during the last quarter of the nineteenth century there has come complexity in all its branches. Type has been wondrously multiplied, inks are in greater profusion, and varieties of paper have rapidly multiplied. The good printer of today needs to know the history of the evolution of type, ink, and paper, if he hopes to be able to cope successfully with the problems facing him.

One reason for this particularity of knowledge is the tendency of the laity to study the technical phases of printing. Type founders have courted the attention of large consumers of printed matter and of large advertisers, and the lay knowledge of type has led to a like result regarding paper. So that it at present happens that the printer's patron is able to dictate the style of typography he desires, and the quality and tint of paper he prefers. This predicates knowledge on the part of the printer; and in the case of paper it necessitates expert knowledge. Type is type, speaking somewhat loosely, and, whatever the crotchet a consumer of printing may get into his head it is not likely to cost more than about so much a pound. It is otherwise with paper, and generally it is more the color, texture, and appearance the patron wishes than the intrinsic value, and the printer must make a choice that shall satisfy the artistic exigencies of the case, as well as consider its financial aspects. One paper may be unsuited for a particular piece of work, and another of the same tint, weight, and price may be exactly suitable; and the reason may lie in so obscure a cause as the peculiar process of manufacture, or the chemical nature of material used by certain paper mills, or a slight variation in finish that may affect ink in a different manner.

A bright and observing printer inevitably becomes more or less versed in paper. He handles it continually, and cannot avoid recognizing certain more evident differences. What is learned in this way is good knowledge, but it takes a long time to get a comprehensive acquaintance with paper, and there has not in the meantime been built up that flawless reputation for good work which all printers regard as the very best capital.

The printer who knows about paper knows about its history, its composition, and the methods of manufacture. To him wood-pulp paper is not all the same, and he knows what he means when he speaks of "all rag" or "handmade." He knows that paper made wholly of wood varies in goodness according as it is made by this or that process—mechanical wood, soda, or sulphite; and knows that "all rags" may be all cotton, or all linen, or a combination of rags, or a combination of wood and rags, or indeed all wood, or some vegetable fiber not specified. It is not the mere exhibition of this sort of knowledge that particularly signifies; it is that it adds greatly to the printer's power to execute good work, as it places him in a position to select the most suitable paper, and insures his reputation. It enables him to execute a piece of work intended to endure a long time in a manner that will preserve its beauty, so that it will not fade or turn a dirty brown or yellow color, as well as to make his paper play its legitimate rôle as the most important inflexible art element he will usually find it necessary to deal with. A knowledge of paper in this thorough sense is even more desirable if a printer presumes to arrogate to himself the title and qualities of an artist. It is scarcely too radical to assert that the esthetics of printing depend for exemplification more upon paper than upon typography. It has been said that type, ink, and paper go to the making of good printing. This formula may be reversed and made to read paper, ink, and type, since so much of the effect of decorative printing depends upon the paper and the ink. If these two harmonize properly it remains that the type must not interfere but must play the negative rôle of conformity. It is the paper that is selected first, then the ink, and lastly the typography is brought into the scheme. Typography, as an ornate art, has dwindled, and the skilled constructor of wonderful effects with types and rule is no longer esteemed in the job room. The arbiter of style sits in the counting-room, and turns the leaves of the paper and type specimen books before the critical eyes of the patron. The job is built upon a paper sample, and the designer sees it completed in his mind before he sends it to the compositor.

Style

STYLE is that subtle atmosphere pervading literary, artistic and handicraft work that suggests the cultivated personality of the author. It is not a usual nor a clear conception of style to consider the term as applicable to inferior work. The word, as used to designate quality, has come to mean positive and recognizable merit, and generally also that indefinite but powerfully distinctive merit indicating individuality.

The word is used somewhat in this sense, though more broadly, in descriptive art nomenclature, as when the style of a Rubens or of a Titian is spoken of; and in art it often appears that the word is used more commonly to designate a school or a genre of painting, than to point to the work of any particular person of the present or the recent past. Yet it is noted that whenever an artist is able to attract favorable attention through the exercise of talents markedly his own, he is at once credited with a style that is distinctively and peculiarly his. It is quite fair and just therefore to consider that style in printing means that quality of beauty or distinction which is to be directly referred to the printer, rather than those meritorious qualities that owe their existence to careful following of established rules and principles, concerning which all printers have, or may have, a working knowledge. There are some printers whose work is so redolent of a peculiar style as to be recognizable to observing persons; and such work has a quality that may almost be said to be narrow. The possessor of a style pronounced enough to have attracted attention is also usually limited in his range; is, in fact, an exponent of his own peculiar style and is but little else.

Style does not absolutely involve excellence; only a distinctive individuality. That individuality may produce printed work that may be wholly bad, or it may be the hall mark of a supreme excellence. This is the technical meaning of the word. In usage the word style is generally understood to imply excellence, and a high grade and peculiarly distinctive excellence. The derivation of the word is suggestive of the accepted appreciation of its scope. It is the Latin name for an iron pen, but it has come to signify not only the art that wields the pen but it is applied to the whole range of the productive activities of man; to music, painting, architecture, sculpture, dancing, acting, tennis and baseball playing; to burglary and picking of pockets, and to printing.

In printing, style is an element of value, and may be accorded as careful attention as is given to the type outfit, to the presses, or to the employes. We can perhaps think of half a dozen printers who have made great reputations and considerable fortunes through having a style that appealed singularly to purchasers of printed matter. What is there in the work of Mr. De Vinne's press that gives the name a distinct value? Why do publishers announce in their advertisements that certain books are printed by De Vinne? Mr. De Vinne's style is valuable to him and to the publishers who employ him to make books for them.

Probably there is not an intelligent printer who may read this who does not recognize the value of style in printing, and who does not, more or less seriously, struggle to acquire for himself a distinctive style, and chiefly because he knows that the possession of a style that appeals to the buyers of printed matter is almost the only sure means of gaining new clients and holding old ones, and obtaining profit-making prices. While there are many printers who will be inclined to scout the idea that the possession of a style of their own would be of financial advantage to them, it is a fundamental element in success. There needs must be some diggers of ditches, hewers of wood and drawers of water, and it is probably true that the great bulk of printing will continue to be done by workmen, a small proportion of it by artisans, and an almost infinitesimal portion by artists. Nevertheless, there is a gravitation toward the artisan class, and from it to the sparse company of the artist printers.

"The only way," says an acute literary critic, "to get a good style is to think clearly." That is in literature.

In printing, the only way to get a good style is to know thoroughly. Yet it is not all to know. The knowledge must be expressed, and it must be expressed in a manner agreeable to those to whom printed matter is to appeal. They do not always know the point of view of the printer, even if he has a style that is admirable. So his style must, after all, be subordinate to clearness and comprehensibility.

In a piece of printing it is necessary to bring out "the extreme characteristic expression" of the central motive. That is, if the piece of printing is intended to promote the sale of a certain substance or article it is desirable that all the suggestive power residing in the types be brought into play to drive the motive home. This is however a secondary quality of style. The primary quality is that which attracts the eye, and style for the printer may be limited to those qualities that do most attract the eye quickly and agreeably.

The secondary literary constituent of style, which is harmony, takes first rank in printing. The three essentials of printing style may be generalized as knowledge, harmony, and expressiveness. In literature they are thought, expressiveness, and harmony, or melody, as some have it. The greatest of these is, of course, knowledge—knowledge of the fundamentals which go to the making of the best printing.

It is not possible to teach style. It is almost as impossible to acquire style. This seems like a paradox, but a paradox is not always a symbol of hopelessness. Style must be born in a man—style in any art or profession. "Style," a writer has recently said, "is gesture—the gesture of the mind and of the soul." We can eliminate the last clause, and call style in printing the gesture of the mind, the evidence of the amount and degree of knowledge possessed by the mind, tempered, arranged, given distinction, by the born talent, aptitude, or whatever it may be termed, which is the seed germ of style. We do not hesitate to accept the obvious theory that artists are born, not made. Some claim for printing that it is an art. Why then should we hesitate to admit that a printer capable of cultivating and expressing a genuine style must depend upon something other than mere knowledge; something deeper and more subtle than knowledge, which is able to mould knowledge into style?

Style, in the highest sense, is given to but few, and we cannot hope that printers will be more favored, in proportion, than the practitioners of other graphic arts. But they may be as highly favored, if they avail themselves of the opportunities for culture that are open to them, as they are open to other artists, and not otherwise. While it is not to be expected that the printing art will produce Morrises or Bradleys with great profuseness, it is to be frankly admitted that in the grade next below—the grade of talent, that is, as distinguished from the grade of genius—there is not found the high average of attainment among printers that rules in other graphic arts. The reason is as obvious as the fact: Printers are not students, in the sense that painters, etchers, engravers, illustrators, and even photographers, are students. Printers (the progressive ones) have in recent years become close observers and good imitators, but there are few who have attempted to qualify themselves for original work by thorough study of those principles of graphic art that vitally control printing. The artist, in any other line than printing, comes to the practice of his art only after prolonged study and mastery of the principles and the laws governing it. Not so with the printer.

The time has arrived when eminence in printing means much more than good work along existing lines. It means a radical departure and the full recognition of the power and value of art in printing. We have been rather hesitant in accepting this word, art, as applying legitimately to printing, and we have been hesitating merely because we have seen the term so freely and ignorantly applied to work that merited no better name than archaic; to work that, while it usually possessed the common virtues of good mechanical execution, was wholly deficient in those qualities which fairly entitled it to be called artistic. But we must put away this prejudice against an innocent and needed term, and boldly reclaim it from the philistines. We must reinstate in the public mind, and in our own minds, the thing and the name that fittingly describes the thing. We must make art printing mean art printing.

Style should be the goal of the printer who cherishes hopes of distinction or of wealth. We have said that style is born in a man, not acquired by him. This is true, if we consider the highest development of style. But we are all capable of greatly improving our style by study. We cannot improve upon it in any other way. It is almost useless for us to observe the good work of others, for this purpose. We must go beyond that. The first step is to keenly realize the need. We are on a par with every other person who wishes to truly understand any art. We cannot arrive at that understanding by merely wishing it. There is no understanding of art except through study of art.

We may spend a lifetime looking at the great paintings of the world and then know so little about them as to appreciate but a tithe of the rich store of culture and pleasure they hold in reserve for us. We may cultivate a taste for paintings by putting ourselves frequently under their influence, as we may build up a taste for literature by strenuous reading. But knowledge, as distinguished from acquaintance, gives us a very different conception of a painting, or a piece of sculpture, or an example of any form of art, and reveals to us new beauties. So it is in printing. We cannot do good color printing unless we understand color as an artist understands it; we cannot get the best results from a halftone engraving unless we understand tone, light and shade, and values, as an artist understands them. We are not sure of our ground with regard to a page of plain type matter unless we know something conclusive about the fundamentals of art.

We cannot take one pronounced step toward acquiring style until we realize the need, the vital need, of a good foundation knowledge of art—not in a historical sense, but in a technical sense—for the technique of printing that is better than good.

The Binding

IT is a pity that bookbinding and printing have drifted so far apart, since they are so intimately related. A good book cannot be produced without the coöperation of both crafts, and that coöperation ought to be of a much closer nature. The printing and the binding of a book should be done by artists or craftsmen actuated by a unity of purpose and effort similar to the unity that must prevail in the book if it is to express anything worthy. In the production of books of a high excellence it is necessary that the binding shall chord with the general nature as expressed through the printing and as fixed by the literary body. This result can only be assured if the printers and the binders work in close harmony. When it is manifestly present in the book of today it is necessary to assume that the agreeable result follows the effects of some influence outside of printers and binders, brought strongly to bear upon each, rather than the result of a harmonious understanding of the artistic proprieties of the case by either the printer or the binder. Binding has a double significance: It is essentially artistic, and emphatically a mechanical process. In its artistic phase it rivals printing; it is considered to be quite apart from printing, in fact, since there is a pretty decided cult in binding that takes no cognizance of typography or of literary character. With this collector's estimate of bindings we are not here concerned. The desire to cheapen production has led to serious deterioration in the quality of binding, of the ordinary library editions of books, during the past century. Machine methods, unobjectionable when used upon very cheap books but disastrous to the lasting quality of library books, have obtained an undesirable vogue, and they are so capable of cleverly simulating good work that they have been a very active agent in the decay of good binding practice. The results of the more recent binding methods are extremely lamentable, and those results have but partially made themselves manifest. The next generation, and the generations after the next, will suffer for the sins of the binders of the books issued during the last half of the nineteenth century. The twentieth century may achieve no more creditable record, but the sinning will be in the light and will not be due to ignorance. The English Society of Arts charged a special committee with the task of investigating the cause of the decay in bindings, and the report of this committee may be one impulse urging publishers to require better workmanship and better methods. This committee formulated five specifications against prevailing methods, each of which constitutes a defect of a radical nature recognizable and curable only by bookbinders or experts in bookbinding. Books are, this committee found, sewn on too few and too thin cords; the slips are pared down too much and are not always firmly enough laced into the boards; the use of hollow backs is condemned; headbands are not sufficiently strong to hold the leather of the back against the strain of taking the book from the shelf; leather used is often far too thin; leather is wetted and stretched to such a point that little strength is left to resist wear and tear.

It must be noted in extenuation that at least one of the counts in this indictment may be partially condoned, upon the ground that the fault crept into bookbinding practice with the intent to facilitate the reading of the book and not to cheapen its production. The hollow back was adopted for the twofold purpose of allowing the book to be opened easily and flatly and to preserve the tooling and gilding on the back. This form of back need not be always reckoned as bad. It is quite possible to bind a book well and use the hollow back, and it is extremely easy to use the hollow back to cover sins that ought not to be condoned in a binding.

The life of a book depends upon its binding. The leading idea in planning a binding for a good book should therefore be to strive for strength, durability, and convenience. To beautify a book in its binding should be the secondary motive. But the idea of beauty, through harmony and the application of elementary art precepts, may always be considered with the strictly utilitarian processes, and the book may be brought into close accord with the requirements of art without any strain for art efforts being apparent nor any economical or mechanical purpose being strained or perverted. This can be effected by arranging the binding to tone with the literary and typographic motives, and studying to have all details harmonious—such as the lettering on the side and back; the design of the stamp for the cover, if there be a stamp; the material for the cover, its texture and its color, etc.

It is manifestly impossible to put into print specific directions for the binding of a book to bring it within the meaning of the term "artistic" while it does not depart from the ordinary in quality or form. It is quite easy to perceive however that for a book of a certain literary quality a binding consisting of a buckram back and paper sides is exactly appropriate, while a cloth binding with a gilt stamp is obviously not harmonious. If the title-stamp on the back of a book is made of type unlike that used for the title-page there is a jarring note that might easily have been avoided. The motive of a book should extend its influence to, and envelope, every process necessary for its completion; it should be as apparently in control of every detail of the visible binding as of the typography, the format, and the paper. It produces an agreeable impression upon the reader if he discovers this artistic unity in a book he hopes to extract literary profit or enjoyment from—if the typography, the format, the paper, and the binding all tone to the same key, and that key in harmony with the literary motive.

This much of art is possible for all bindings. When they rise above this mere expression of harmony, of unity, there is a widely different question involved. Then there must be art for art's sake, rather than art for the book's sake; and of bindings that are in and of themselves works of art we have for the present nothing to say.

As to exactly what constitutes a proper binding for a given book there may be differences of opinion, especially if the inquiry be pushed so far as to involve questions of art, or questions concerning the artistic qualities of harmony and unity. There are however certain broad lines which may be indicated within which worthy bindings must be brought, leaving plenty of latitude for individuality in taste and in judgment. What these basic requirements are is perfectly known to practical bookbinders and to publishers; to many printers as well. They should be as familiar to the lay mind, and every book should have printed somewhere in it a clear statement of the specifications of its binding. Its typography is visible; so is its format and its paper. The vital parts of its binding are concealed, from the expert as from the tyro, and every purchaser of an ordinary book stands to lose heavily if the foundations of its binding are not honestly laid.

The specifications for the binding of a fine book should show, then, that the cover material is all leather of some one of the approved sorts and properly manufactured, sheets carefully folded, single leaves guarded round the sections next to them, all plates guarded, guards sewn through, and no pasting or overcasting; end papers sewn on and made of good paper, board papers of good quality of paper or vellum; edges to be trimmed and gilt before sewing, or left uncut; sewing to be with ligature silk around five bands of best sewing cord; back to be as nearly flat as possible without forcing it and without danger of its becoming concave in use; boards to be of the best black millboard, and the five bands laced in through two holes; headbands to be worked with silk on strips of vellum or catgut or cord, with frequent tiedowns, and "set" by pieces of good paper or leather glued at head and tail; lettering to be legible, in harmony with the typography of the book or with the decorations; decorations such as may be wished.

These skeletonized specifications may be modified in some particulars if they are to be applied to grades of books below the best, but great care and good judgment must be exercised to guard against an extent of deterioration which will bring the book below its standard of utility and beauty. For library books, for example, the covers may be half leather or any of the several serviceable cloths; the end papers may dispense with the board papers; the edges may be cut guillotine and colored instead of gilt, or the top only may be gilt; the sewing may be done with unbleached thread and the tapes may be reduced to four of unbleached linen; the boards may be of split gray stock or of strawboard with black board liner, and the tapes may be attached to portion of waste sheet inserted between the boards; the headbands may be omitted and cord substituted, or they may be worked with thread or vellum.

Specifications

The paper in this book is French handmade, 16 × 20–29, imported by the Japan Paper Company of New York, and catalogued as No. 333.

The type is a liberal modification of the Caslon, 12 point. It was designed and cast by the Boston branch of the American Type Founders Company, and had never been used until set for this book.

The binding is according to the specifications of the Society of Arts, of London. The sheets are folded with special care, end papers are made with zigzag and sewn on, edges are uncut, signatures are sewn with unbleached thread over three unbleached linen tapes, back left nearly square, boards of the best black millboard, covers of imported marbled paper, and the backs of art vellum, with paper label. The binding was executed by the regular force of workmen and in the regular routine of commercial work.

The composition of the type was by a journeyman and an apprentice, and the presswork was done on a half super royal Colt's Armory press. No attempt has been made to execute the work in other than the ordinary manner, with ordinary appliances and ordinary workmen. All the material is such as is regularly carried in stock by dealers.

Milton Keynes UK
Ingram Content Group UK Ltd.
UKHW030627061024
449204UK00004B/259